THE PORTAGE POETRY SERIES

SERIES TITLES

Lost Cathedral
Hannah Rodabaugh

An Introduction to Error
Deirdre Lockwood

Wildfire
Corie Rosen

Pandora's Prairie
Katherine Hoerth

How We Argue
Sharon Rose-Kourous

The Weather of Our Names
Cal Freeman

Temporary Shelters
Grant Clauser

tic tic tic
Heidi Seaborn

And the Heart Will Not Quicken
Russell Thorburn

Exile Is Home
Elvis Alves

Even the Sky
Kevin Thomason

The Underdream
Aiyana Masla

Dining on Salt: Four Seasons of Septets
Wayne Lee

Torrential
Jayne Marek

Users with Access: New and Selected Poems
Brandon Krieg

Flu Season
Katie Kalisz

No Trouble Staying Awake
Teresa Scollon

Another Native Tongue
Susan Riley Clarke

Catch & Release
Lauren Crawford

Steelhead
Lauren K. Carlson

The Coronation of the Ghost
Benjamin Gantcher

The Stone Tries to Understand the Hands
Susannah Sheffer

Red Camaro
Dwaine Rieves

Where Babies Come From
Ori Fienberg

Cuttings
Hannah Dow

Forgive the Animal
Sarah Pape

Love as Invasive Species
Ellen Kombiyil

They Were Horrible Cooks
Allison Whittenberg

The New Life
Wendy Wisner

Restoring Prairie
Margaret Rozga

Table with Burning Candle
Julia Paul

A Bright Wound
Sarah A. Etlinger

The Velvet Book
Rae Gouirand

Listening to Mars
Sally Ashton

Glitter City
Bonnie Jill Emanuel

The Trouble with Being a Childless Only Child
Michelle Meyer

Happy Everything
Caitlin Cowan

Dear Lo
Brady Bove

When is a celebration of life a requiem? When is a love song a eulogy? "Every poem an epitaph," wrote T. S. Eliot more than eight decades ago, although in 1942, when he wrote that phrase, the very idea of concern, if not fear, for the future of the planet and that which lives upon it, hadn't really dawned on much of anyone yet. Now, a quarter of the way through the twenty-first century, Hannah Rodabaugh is viscerally aware of the nearness of absolute earthly extinction. If what she writes in *Lost Cathedral* is a requiem, it is also that oldest of songs, about a love that will somehow never end.

—ROBERT WRIGLEY
Winner of the Pacific Northwest Book Award
author of *Box*

Lost Cathedral sings of the "wild emptiness" of an earth increasingly emptied out. Bemoaning the many means by which we bipeds "walk our saws into the sea," these masterful works celebrate some of our most treasured relatives: the great forest giants, the mule deer, the Galapagos penguins. Alternately ecstatic and anguished, the poems detail the twinned processes of cherishing and grieving; moving forward, moving backward; keening and reclaiming. This book is marvelous. Its courageous intensity amplifies our common will to tend life's every seed.

—DIANE RAPTOSH
author of *American Amnesiac*

Lost Cathedral stands as a reminder to collect ourselves, to enter stillness, to sit with nature. Hannah Rodabaugh's careful attention creates timeless meaning in these urgent times. This collection reaches beyond words, each line gathering momentum, while demanding quiet engagement. Hannah's sharp observation, wisdom, and curiosity, hold hope and beauty as an act of resistance. Here, we remember that poetry, too, is an act of resistance.

—REBECCA EVANS
author of *Safe Handling*

What is there to say when nature has become a killing floor and you're part of the gang of thieves responsible? In these rich, verdant, blisteringly clear-eyed poems, Hannah Rodabaugh bears witness to what we've lost.

—CATHERINE WAGNER
author of *Nervous Device*

Lost Cathedral is equal parts ecopoetics and elegy, as these deeply-researched poems reanimate the creatures eradicated by our long history of dominance over the natural world. On behalf of these extinct animals and ecosystems, Rodabaugh laments "all the worlds we couldn't save. The words we could have said to them unspoken...." In an earnest appeal to stop our hubris from finishing what it started centuries ago, those words are being spoken now.

—EMILY PITTINOS
author of *The Last Unkillable Thing*

Working against "embellishment," *Lost Cathedral* proposes a meticulous, entangled poetics of extinction and complicity, grounded in questions of home. As Hannah Rodabaugh writes, in an on-going archive of instants or glimpses that never rise to the level of perception or encounter: "Sit in an empty field/ and ask yourself/what is missing."

—BHANU KAPIL

With the lyricism of a poet and the precision of a documentarian, Hannah Rodabaugh turns a fierce mirror on the forces that have deprived whole species of their existence: colonialism, anthropocentrism, and plain old everyday hubris. Come gently tend the trail of this searching, powerful book.

—CATHERINE BROADWALL
author of *Fulgurite*

In *Lost Cathedral*, Hannah Rodabaugh offers a clear-sighted view of a world where the nonhuman recedes. Drawing on a quiet awareness of extinction's long history, Rodabaugh's poetry gives language to the desperate search for connection in a transforming landscape and the heartrending echoes of loss when wild beings, their songs, and thus parts of ourselves, vanish. This carefully crafted collection, rendered with beautiful language, reminds us of what we stand to lose when we stop listening.

—CMARIE FUHRMAN
author of *Salmon Weather: Writing from the Land of No Return*

Lost Cathedral

poems

HANNAH RODABAUGH

CORNERSTONE PRESS
UNIVERSITY OF WISCONSIN-STEVENS POINT

Cornerstone Press, Stevens Point, Wisconsin 54481
Copyright © 2025 Hannah Rodabaugh
www.uwsp.edu/cornerstone

Printed in the United States of America.

Library of Congress Control Number: 2025941891
ISBN: 978-1-968148-16-4

Cornerstone Press titles are produced in courses and internships offered by the
Department of English at the University of Wisconsin–Stevens Point.

DIRECTOR & PUBLISHER   EXECUTIVE EDITORS
Dr. Ross K. Tangedal   Jeff Snowbarger, Freesia McKee

EDITORIAL DIRECTOR   SENIOR EDITORS
Brett Hill   Paige Biever, Eva Nielsen, Reilly Crous

PRESS STAFF
Leo Poskoum, Ryleigh Miller, Brianna Loving, Aja Wolley, Abby Paulsen, Sophie McPherson,
Sam Bjork, Madison Schultz, Autumn Vine

ALSO BY HANNAH RODABAUGH:

The Leonids

We Don't Bury Our Dead When Our Dead Are Animals

With Words: Verse in Concordance

We Traced The Shape Of Our Loss To See Your Face

CONTENTS

Lost Cathedral

Lost Object   3

Lost Sound (Spotted Owl)   5

The Forest Took You Over   7

Listen Well (Sound Map)   10

Mule Deer   11

Terra Incognita   13

Silent Forest   15

Giant Redwood   17

The Animal Outside Us   19

How They Met Themselves   20

Lost Giants of the Pacific Coast   21

Old-Growth in Decline   22

Leave Things Alone   25

Last Prayer of the Logger   26

Historical Graffiti   28

Lost Animals

I.

The Animals of Lost and Found   39

Laughing Owl, 1909   40

Laughing Owl, 1909   41

Greater Short-Tailed Bat, 1965   42

Thylacine, 1933   43

Thylacine, 1933   44

London Zoo, 1864   45

Kaua'i 'Ō'ō, 1987   48

Priorities | Memento Mori   49

Mamo, 1892   50

Daguerreotype, 1892   52

Daguerreotype, 1832   54

Last Sighting of the Dodo   55

Pacific Islands Under New Management   59

Natural History Museum   61

Daguerreotype, 1926   64

II.

Pigeon of Passage   69

Triptych on a Passenger Pigeon in 1886 Chicago   70

The Mouth of Extinction   76

Extinction 101   78

Victorian Menagerie   79

White Rhino, 2018   80

Black Rhino, 2011   81

Stool Pigeons   82

A Market Economy   85

Last Flight of the Wild Blue Pigeon (to Martha)   86

Lost Animals   87

Vestiary   89

Martha at the Smithsonian   91

Elegy for *Ectopistes Migratorius*   92

Last Flight of the Wild Blue Pigeon   94

Notes   97

Acknowledgments   101

Lost Cathedral

Lost Object

When you lose something here,
you lose it forever. You drop it,

and the trees trap it, or the wind
pulls it away from you. Another

valley over, your lost object twists
between trees, its twine breaking,

amber light flowing over the trunks
like something oily. When you

lose something, you believe it can
be followed or found, that some

things can be clung to or claimed
when you hold your hands out,

but instead, they disappear. Whole
worlds are lost. The forest is thick

with snow-green vegetation, wet
air in a state of undress, mist in

a heavy beard of white. The trees
feel fully indecipherable, how

things stay hidden, twisting out
of view when you strain your

eyes to look. Dogwood and pine,
piles of slanted logs flecked with

the bilious capillaries of lichen,
hiding what might be yours

(or also someone else's) until you
can't stop looking. Bell-shaped

manzanita blossoms under heavy
crowns of murky green arrive slowly

in front of you. The forest is all
sharp angles, geometric sunlight.

The bristling trunks close in, a kind
of vertigo. They've stolen you,

and you're guessing at where
you've been or where you're going.

Lost Sound (Spotted Owl)

Sit in an empty field
                            and ask yourself
what is missing.

What bird
           flower
                      bee
                         tree

is gone now that should
                        be here?
Wait to hear the
                 answer from the wind
that tells you
                 how to look,
its empty howling.
                    Let it
fill you
               with a
wet, hollow feeling
                   until you, too,
are green and growing.
                 Then
ask yourself,
               what
lived here once
               that also
felt this wind
               come alive inside
of them?
               What rare plant
felt its
               frosted buds
grow cold
               from a
spring storm
               of hail

```
                    against
the mountain
                    tinged with green?
What
                    soft sounds
of night
once
                    called out
under the
                    high-mooned
sky
                    from
deep within
the rushing of
                    these endless
waves of
                    fir?
```

The Forest Took You Over

1.

If you stand
still long enough,
the moss will
grow over you.

It will cover you
like a great sea.

If you imagine
you are a tree,
your arms out
like branches,

the wind
moving you,
the rain
washing over you,

when you look down,
you will be greener.

Moss will
cling to you
like the flowing hair
of sunlight.

If you don't
believe me,
go deep into the heart
of the forest.

Let night
pass over you
full of dark wingbeats,

let the day
fleck you
with rain and snow.

Stand still
and tall
in the forest,

and wait to see
how green you get.

2.

I know a man who fell asleep in the forest, and the forest took him over. In his sleep, it absorbed him. When he woke, he was a madrone tree, his bark peeling like the hair of an orange. His clothes had turned to moss, eyebrows tinged a yellow-green. His arms were full of nests, wrens and chickadees swarming him like gnats. His teeth were gray-white stalactites glowing like a cloud with the moon behind it. He tried to speak, and bats flew out (one stuck to his uvula making him clear and clear his throat). Now he stands somewhere in the forest, his long beard trailing, his body swaying in the sighing wind. He's forgotten everything. If you find him, see if you can call him back. You'll try, but he'll just keep swallowing the light, his body a bright green star.

Listen Well (Sound Map)

If you want to know a place's
imbuing wildness, you must
listen to it speak. Sit where
the world folds slowly
around you and wait for
your ears to turn outward.
Water is always there, an
unambiguous dripping on the
vegetation around you: bees a
broken-sounded sawing above
tapping trillium and tawny ginger—
the wind's soft breathing
creaking the firs' heavy mantle,
billowing branches above the
nuthatch's tinny trumpet.
Below you streams a river's
staticky hum (from far away
a wren's voice also bubbling).
If you walk along this copse,
you'll note the wingbeats
of a goshawk or see the
night-dark raven croaking
from within a sea of pine.
Or you'll hear nothing,
where the forest is silent
like it's nursing secret hurt
or hiding something fearful.
If you listen hard enough,
you'll hear the green things
growing all around you, hear
the yellow buds of flowers
unclasping loudly, see the moss
march forward over every stone.

Mule Deer

Each deer
is a kōan—
                a half-hidden
                untruth truth,
a gentle,
empty expression

                of wisdom
                on their face:
the silence
just before
                a thought
                or just after.
Each deer
is an enigma—
                their blank
                faces housing
a delicate
ambiguity
of helplessness,

                this delicacy
                we use.
We use
the weak
                for everything
                but their wisdom.

We find the
smallest place

                that we
                can fit them
and then fit
them in.
                We find them
                irreparably dull.

We've made
them into
ourselves.

Terra Incognita

I don't know if a forest
has rights, if its life
or the lives it holds

are more important
than mine. I just know
if it was gone, I would

miss it. I would miss
its wild emptiness,
its ability to be somewhere

unknowable to me,
miss that there is
a place carved out

I cannot trace. We are
always happiest
when approaching

a form of understanding—
the moment before
a thought becomes

a thought—how you
can't see it until you
see it. I want forests

to be this uninhabitable,
to have this kind
of wisdom, living

on the gnarled edge
of what can be said,
what can be known.

A forest does not
exist just for me to
add to my knowledge

(a forest is not here
to mold into how
you've molded you).

I can think of no
higher honor to
bestow on any

copse of trees than
to know, to be aware,
of my unimportance

to all that's in it.
There is no higher
honor I could

give than for it
to live life without
ever knowing me,

so, when I'm gone,
I was unknown,
I was the mystery.

Silent Forest

A forest
is silent
when there is

nothing left
in it
to sing.

Imagine,
clear air
of early morning

(bright &
shivering canopy,
dark solemnity

of trunk)
and nothingness
below it,

no woodpecker's
soft staccato
or thrush's

liquid flute.
An earth
emptied out

is an earth
emptied out
and sadness

serves no purpose,
won't put
those melodies back—

lives just
can't be saved
with good intentions.

Giant Redwood

Your first thought when you see
a giant redwood—head in the clouds,

feet in a sea of ferns—is how many
yous across it is, how many *yous*

will fit in there. The far back and
not so far back—how many pasts,

how many futures? Is it living a life
for *all of you?* The distant past not

so distant here: the past still present
in a tree somewhere, the past still

living in a tree. Or how you know
you're old when things grow over

you, breath of moss condensing,
lichen coral reef (bark in ribbons

of baleen, trunks of heat-curled hair).
Or how time speeds up on different

parts of you: your body hollowed
out, our biggest echo chamber,

your crown still in the sky, beating
heart of green. Your last thought

when you see a giant redwood is
how few escaped us, nothing certain,

survival not certain anywhere.
A bird forgets its nesting site at

the swan of summer, a vole forgets
its burrow, we forget time traps us

(a hole filled with distractions),
but a tree will keep remembering.

The Animal Outside Us

Classification is not a form
of knowing; naming is not
a body knowledge, is still
a thing we cannot know.
The mystery of others,

that they are always other,
the animal outside us even
though we are an animal.
We think we have the only
bead on feeling, on an internal

monologue, that we are the
only *I* here, the only realized
self, and we use this to create
an atrophy, a legal, fiscal state
where we are the only legal

entity, the only one entitled
to respect, until respect is
crooked land use, respect is
logging trees, walking our saws
along the spine of the earth

to walk our saws into the sea.
Respect is using this world
where this world needs us least,
the bare earth creased with
mines, the silver specks of cars.

How They Met Themselves

There's something primeval in a place
where trees the size of skyscrapers
swab the sky. Here you may be cursed
when you meet a crooked doppelgänger
in the woods. Worlds may fall apart.
Seams of light may start to unravel.
Unearthly light, this atmospheric glowing,
will seek to woo you. Trunks dipped
in moss will carry the light like lines
of silver. Rocks will wield bearded faces
in humid green. Stumps the size of cars
will chew out tiny specks of plants
within their rusting cores of red. Frozen
waves of mushrooms will eke out under
maidenhair, their leaves unrolling as
waves of wine-dark sea. Greenness
with light behind it like greenness singing.
You'll expect and not expect something
to happen. The back of your neck will
tense like something watched. This world
was set in motion long before you; a great
drama is playing out, and you're butting in.
You'll start to feel unmade, until you're
only a thought in the vibrating skin of
something else, until you feel half-formed.
You're here before the world was still,
when silence made the earth into its terror—
the valley shaking apart as skeins of clouds,
lining the jagged peaks in green and gold,
the light like something sharp, unholy reliquary,
bruising the white sky above in jets of fir.

Lost Giants of the Pacific Coast

You read a book about the last great forest giants, the last great thunderbolts, a perplexity carving the earth as printed paper—a book on missing forest made from forest. A gravestone for the living made from the dead, mourning a thing by mourning its mirror image, as if grief can be transferred, but grief cannot be transferred. We always mourn the thing we mourn alone. Night still brings its unending silence over us whatever names it still may hold.

Old-Growth in Decline

All great trees

(with names
so big
& mighty)

are gone
from here.

Here we name
individuals

because
individuals are
what's left.

They are the
bright-branched

remnants
of centuries
of logging

where men
walked their saws
almost to the sea

sharp heart
of green—

*just 'cause
your life
matters here*

*doesn't mean
it matters
anywhere.*

These remnants
wear our
ancient crowns

& these
we give
grand names—

      like *genesis*
      and *general*

      titan or
      lost monarch

      as if the names
      carry the past
      with them—

      gone, but
      not forgotten.

Walking
under them

we call
them some
earthly cathedral—

      how each
      tall top

      brushes wind
      into the sky,
each body
like the

buttressed rib
of a great whale,

      how they
      punctuate

      the earth
      like a thunderbolt.

It is a
branch deep-
rooted in us

                    that the lesser
                    be impressed
                    by what is less,

that what
we see

                    is what we
                    can only see,

that we
can stand
before an
emptied forest

                    with its feet
                    of clay and stone
where once
a golden
statue stood
                    (a Colossus
                    with its
                    bronzy head)
and still
we'll sing
its praises
                    this we will
                    Ozymandias.
How easy
it is to praise
something

once it is
already gone.

Leave Things Alone

The best way to love a wild
animal is to leave it alone,
to move away from its nest,
harsh calls of alarm in the

sky above you. The best way
to love a wild animal is to
care from a far distance, the
light swirling around you as

you observe a falcon from
far away. The world doesn't
belong to you. The space
around an animal is its own.

The best animal encounter
is the one that didn't happen
because you kept such a far
distance that it didn't know

that you were here. If you love
something, you let it be itself,
you let the world shape it with-
out you. You leave it alone.

Last Prayer of the Logger

Each day, you do not pray for life,
you pray for life's removal.
You pray for the removal of others.
You pray for forests to end, but also
for them to be endless, a form of
always waving goodbye. You pray
to fell monsters, that you might not
be consumed, that you might stand
over their ancient backs, grime on
your face, bones almost incandescent,
bright as a blue whale birthed
by the sea, then heavy on the back
of your cart, the smell of oil and
cedar in the air, a dizzying fragrance.
You pray for someone to keep interceding
on your behalf, that you can keep
emptying the world out. You pray
to see sunrises unclouded by branches,
the fresh green earth held up by a
heart of blue. The fresh green earth:
the dawn, a welcome arm above it.
You pray to see horizons unobscured,
a collapsing viewpoint, the broken
hearts of tree stumps twisting the earth
beneath you, the sky chewing out
a chasm to hold your deep feeling
like a feather trapped in sedge.
You pray to hear your voice where
the Morse of boreal owls once
wandered, for one voice to be subsumed
by the working sounds of another,
that the forests where you work keep
carrying your name. This is a prayer
for the sky, for an unobstructed view.
The sky rooting you, a kind of
looking up, of always looking away.
This is a prayer for the moon

between the mountains' empty throat,
sky gargling out a stranded web
of silver. This is a prayer that the earth
not become empty by becoming empty,
even if only your name still echoes.

Historical Graffiti

1.

Carbide lanterns and pine-pitch torches
stained the walls a smoky gray. Smeared
arrows of ash show the way through the

chambers' twisted interior. The world
moves slowly here. Above you, heavy
stalactites carved by eons of seeping

rainwater, jagged teeth thick as a
forearm. By lantern, women crawled
on hands and knees in heavy skirts,

men in canvas pants and logging boots,
to stand here in these gleaming caves
of flowstone, stalactites hanging like

the pipes of a spectral organ. They wrote
in loops of lead, scrawling names, dates,
sometimes messages, that blot the walls

along a fixture called Niagara, a cataract
of creamy stone rushing like a waterfall.
Each twist or turn has a name hidden in

it like a tiny memory. The names crowd
around you: brothers, students, friends
who first found the mountain's empty

heart. There are no memories here
that matter. Dissolved calcite keeps
rebuilding, trapping the names under

translucent layers of stone. They'll
soon be covered, both here and not,
an echo and also erased, part of the

deep's nameless history. They'll live
forever where no one can read them.
The stones have no memory. The earth

always replaces. The world keeps you
like walking across waves of sand:
even the wind will remove your steps.

2.

You brought the day in with you, and put it here, there, everywhere, lights threading the ground, illuminating cascades of stone, misshapen features smeared across the walls like ghosts. You brought in ideas of what mattered, of what you should value. You took souvenirs, scraping stalactites hanging from the ceiling like chandeliers, calcite drapery that formed over thousands of years—or left lead signatures that will never wash away. (*Do Not Destroy* you carved into slabs of flowstone above the mouths of missing teeth.) Some marring will be permanent. Others, time will heal. Still, you will keep on leaving your impressions. You want to remember the world with you in it. Outside a cave mouth matted with moss, you carve your initials into the naked green bark of a madrone like you're William Clark carving his name in an alder tree on the mouth of the Columbia River.

3.

You want to remember the world
with you in it, how it's easy to
forget that you're here if no one is
speaking your name. In a cemetery,
you saw how rain erodes each name
from stone until nothing remains,
how even language dies. You want
to remember the world with you
in it. You find a pencil and scrawl
your name onto rocks beside you.
You're underground. The walls
are heather gray under yellow
beams of candlelight. The world
looks melted, pale fingers fringe
the ceiling like oily feathers.
You're finally going to get what
you want. When the world moves
forward, it will move forward
with you. *You've made your mark.*

4.

Sometimes you destroy what you love. You sign your name on the world around you. You mark it until every flower, its every petal, is stained with your name. The icy pink orchid is patterned with your voice like grainy lines of Morse. The birds wear your colors. You're the first dawn trembling with red-gold light, the first word spoken inside the first voice, the stars' slow movement eclipsed by your skin, the moon's slick pattern of slanted light smearing the earth beneath you. You're everywhere, and the world is too small for you. You're everywhere, and you're grasping onto the one thing you can crawl inside of. You write it down. Everywhere the earth fills up with naming like the cold scent from underneath the cedar limbs. You know each separate color, each tiny part, now that you've classified it, given it a tiny heart to beat. Still the earth keeps leaving you behind; it keeps replacing you. You're buried or eroded by time's slow sickle. The pattern of cruelty is to give you a creation that also removes you, how memory always repairs. Your effort to make a deep impression goes unrewarded. The future won't look at you with the same eyes or won't look at you at all.

Lost Animals

I.

The Animals of Lost and Found

It's not so much that they're *lost*, it's that they're *found*,
it's that they're *found* somewhere else:

> *in books, museums, memories, and grainy*
> *photographs (forgettably, the unconscious).*

No substitute for a body, these.

> *A Japanese sculptor makes felt animals for*
> *a lost zoo, tiny figures among plastic plants;*
>
> *a lab attempts to clone from living relatives,*
> *(unpopular, this form of going backwards),*
>
> *their mission statement reads: WE WILL*
> *BRING THEM BACK UNTIL THEY ARE*
> *NO LONGER REMOVABLE FROM US.*

No substitute for a body, these.

Laughing Owl, 1909

Perched in a New Zealand cave, a laughing owl is force-fed small mice by an inland photographer. They want to capture a wild moment by fabricating it. *Who wants to wait for the wilderness to happen?* The owl's body is twisted away from the camera as if to escape it. A mouse hangs from its beak like a dead branch, its refusal to cohabitate any narrative. The cruelty of this juxtaposition, that this is the only photo of the species taken in the wild. *In the wild* meaning *our faulty interpretation of nature,* meaning *the place where we pretend to know wildness.*

Laughing Owl, 1909

We heard it singing and wanted it. We wanted to contain it until it was on a shelf like something to hold inside of us. It exists now in our memories, our artificial impulses. We've replaced its ability to act or to be separate from us. Our world has become its world now that its world is gone, now that it is finally gone. It lives on the musty shelves of some antiquated menagerie, the locked specimen cases that hide behind the walls of every museum like catacombs of the dead. Now we can tell its story. We can tell how we've interpreted it, how we've named it, given it a heart to beat, whenever we mouth its name.

Greater Short-Tailed Bat, 1965

There is only one photograph of you that we
know of in existence. It's 1965. Grimy, a biologist
holds you, your wings distorted behind you, a kill of
stamina folded out of you. That you lived as bats did
before that moment, where in the glare of the camera
flash, you are weakened. That it drained you of any
life you knew up until that moment, where you
look delicate and broken—already extinct.

Thylacine, 1933

Each day, the wind is coolly
in the sky, making weather
patterns; the sun rolls up each
morning in an unearthly red,
but it cannot walk my body

back into the place it came
from, cannot walk my life
back into the Hobart Zoo
where I died from exposure,
a fully-preventable death—

and when I speak to you
what do you expect to come
out of my throat? A whole
torn island ecosystem where
I lay nestled once? Do you

expect a whole lost earth to
fall out of my mouth? Like
Saturn, you devoured all the
living here. You were hungry,
but you also ate too much.

Thylacine, 1933

It's something to see the dead
go so far back into the past,

to see them as an unbroken
chain of *being here*—and to

matter—that the person who
drew your outline in bright

orange paint did not do so
idly. You don't seek to capture

what you don't value, what
you don't love. What happened

that we changed so much—
that we only gave it protected

status two months before its
death, before the last one

gave up its ghost? Its ghost a
simple cave scrawl, gliding

on the rock, still finding ways
to haunt us. In a 1933 film,

we see it just outside the
frame in its cage at the Hobart

Zoo, worlds apart from the
world it inhabited in the wild,

its body an enjambment,
a melismatic moment, as it

reaches toward a shadowy
figure just outside its cage.

London Zoo, 1864

Mirror within a Mirror

I am looking at
photographer Frank Haes' picture of
a man in a top hat
looking at a
quagga[3] that is
staring at the viewer.

My	intent looking at
Frank's	intent looking at
the man's	intent looking at
the animal's	bleary-eyed grief.

As if there is
some knowledge in this
looking.

Is there?

---

[3] An extinct subspecies of zebra.

More or Less

When I look into the quagga's
face now   I see
boredom and   jaded, foreign
        expression
                    splayed open.

What did   a stereoscopic
viewer   see
in   1864?

The quagga was
only a machine   capable
of organism in
                  a cramped
          enclosure?

Or this
animal is
                            every impulse
          too many   like
a woman?

                  An
animal body is only
          too little
or
          too much
          for us.

Human Potential

It was 1864 and everyone trembled. There was a
quagga at   the London Zoo behind a   flimsy fence as
if the quagga had   no exit strategy beyond it. People visited it
in its sharp-cornered enclosure. They weighed in using 19th
century diction about the half-striped, half-roan body. They punted
out *thees*   and *thous* while wearing top hats like coats
of mail. They gave speeches. Mated groups of bitter enemies in
order to attack nations. They were   themselves
ennationed. Everybody lived full   lives in 1864.
Everybody's promise was   opening. The quagga was only
a fountain   displaying promise for   many men
in top hats. With   waiting intention, they listened.

Kaua'i 'Ō'ō, 1987

Where is there a refuge
if not here   in front of you–

the pages you   keep working,
          the magazines you   silently read.

Trapped between   each cell:
          the ghostly wails   of Kaua'i 'Ō'ō.

YouTube clips
          with sordid titles
like *Male Singing*   *to Female That*

                    Will Never Come
about its last
          one-sided duet.
All your
          misplaced anger,   all your grief,

     not at   *we did not save them,*

but that   *they did not*
                    hold their hands
          out to you

     (memories   of the lost'll
seldom carry you)—

     not at their   missing forests,
a refugia   that grew here once

     that truly   was a refuge,
not merely   memories,
          caustic catalogs.

Priorities | Memento Mori

What can I say to apologize for my failings?
What spider or gnat do I kill now, as nuisance,
that will be tomorrow's passenger pigeon or
Carolina parakeet? *They were so numerous*
that they didn't matter—that I didn't learn
names or take pictures. They were not other
enough until extinguished, it took extinction
to make them other to us—now no photos
of the Carolina parakeet exist except two:
one of a bird named Doodles perching next
to a man's mouth, and one which is clearly
doctored. What were people doing with
early cameras besides not taking pictures
of green parakeets in the millions? *Here is*
my mother's photo—she was a lovely corpse.
You are her inheritor—she lives in you—
a question of how we determine if our priorities
are skewed or not. *Should you have taken*
pictures of what you know or what you know
to have value? Is there even a difference?
Everyone's relatives played out in parakeets
at some point, only no one cares about their
bodies. Everyone really into Victorian fad[3]
of taking photos of bodies at funerals while
we struggle to conceive of the landscape
those bodies lived in once. I look at the
doctored picture of a parakeet, and I think
it looks flat—made out of paper—how can
it have been green—yellow—vermillion?
How can life have existed in what we cannot
mention? Asking around the dinner table,
would you like to see our daughter posed with
her siblings? Meanwhile millions of parakeets
are being extinguished like a goodbye game
we play with schoolchildren. What gets to
be remembered has to do with politics. We do
not remember what we ourselves extinguish.

---

[2] Postmortem photography.

Mamo, 1892

In a blurry photograph from 1892,
a man holds a mamo, a Hawaiian

honeycreeper he had caught with
sugar water. It was fated to be a

scientific specimen, one of the last
wild mamos caught living, and his

sleepy grin looks foolish as he holds
the end of something. What do we

do with him—with people like him
in photos of what is lost? Are they

an enemy, a bystander, or both?
(People are sophisticated, no one

caricature.) What do we do with
the good and bad in each person

when we look at photos of people
that are holding an extinct animal

or are touching it mildly? Trying
to name it with their hands, as if

a name will replace the body of
the animal when it disappears,

a way of replacing an animal's lived
experience with our experience of

the animal (flesh memory so vivid
to so many people), until everything

is humanized. The man who holds
the mamo is loving—he is quite

taken with the bird. He caresses
it with his hands until it is erased.

Daguerreotype, 1892

Sometimes I wonder
about the people
who collected specimens

for wealthy individuals
or institutions,
the man who caught

the last wild mamo,
posed for a photograph,
the bird tied to

his finger with string
(long dead memories
unburied) before

preparing it for a
Rothschild's personal
collection. I did not

expect to join him,
to feel his point
of view, but here I am

pacing the river
collecting beetles
for a Harvard entomologist.

Who am I here?
What lives in me now?
Am I remarkable or

the worst? If I inhabit
one man's photo,
his page in history,

whose eyes look out

at me when I study
his face? (When *we*

hold the mamo,
our face's sheer delight,
what do *I* carry

with *you?*) Both species
lost their lives, the beetles
and the mamo, the price

for gaining knowledge.
Knowledge at your expense—
our only leitmotif.

Daguerreotype, 1832

Alexander Wilson, a failed poet & Scottish immigrant, painted each line carefully in *American Ornithology*, a landmark of naturalist painting, our first representation of wild birds. Wilson caught and killed his models, held them still in lifelike poses, only once drew from a live bird, an ivory-billed woodpecker shot near his home in Wilmington, North Carolina. He tried to tame it, left it in his room. When he returned, it had drilled through the walls in a flurry of desperation, fist-sized chunk of plaster missing, white clouds over the bed. The bird was a weatherboard from freedom, a wet green storm of leaves, bellows of humid green, our future and our history tied to it with string. Wilson admired its energy, wouldn't release it; eventually it died of starvation. Naturalists rarely keep an animal before using it for some reason. The bird that broke through walls, bit his hands when he would try to paint, became a series of episodic images noted for their listlessness, missing spit & breath. What's left is the story, a traveler's yarn. The bird's restlessness, its *unconquerable American spirit*, as Wilson called it (a desperation we couldn't conquer), is somehow missing; his words can't breathe life into it any more than his images. Only its crest (an alarming red) carries any flint.

Last Sighting of the Dodo

Unremarkable

By the last sighting of the dodo,
sailors thought it was a mythical
creature. They forgot it had been

real once. They lost their memories
of its wingless body nested on
the beach, until they doomed it

into nothingness. It became a
gesture they made to each other
in passing—a kind of dream

they did not remember upon
waking—so that after a hundred
dwindling years, when they saw

the last one walking toward them,
it troubled them, made them worry
that the earth was spouting out

its monsters, worried what
might next come out of the earth—
how our bright fears come alive

only when we least expect them,
until even seeing it again became
something uncalled for, uncanny

in its jeopardizing quality. Other
species soon followed it into
nothingness, past all their haunted

gestures—a giant tortoise, owl,
flying fox, and parakeet—but by
then the sailors did not notice them

or their absence—how things that
are unreal are often unremarkable
if we tell ourselves enough.

Colonization of Mauritius

Things that are unreal

                  are unremarkable

if you

        tell yourself enough—

until every lost thing

                  is merciless

in its unremarkability.

You go about your day,

               you keep

planting your fields—

               you get used to

things missing,

           lost socks, keys,

whole cultures,

           whole

island ecosystems.

You so little

           troubled yourself

to learn the animals

               on the island

you are colonizing—

their names,

           the things

they called

         each other—

that you never noticed

             that some

were missing.

You feel the world

             moves forward

around you,

          you move forward—
how you're
          no longer
tied to the sea.

You tell yourself
          the world
untroubles islands,
                    so far away
from anywhere
          that matters.

You can't imagine
                    a world
less likely
     to change
in ways
     that hold meaning
to *you*,

     less likely

to hold a future
          that *you*
won't recognize.

Journal Entry

> *We drove them together into one place in such a manner that we
> could catch them with our hands, and when we held one of them by
> its leg, the others came running as fast as they could to its assistance,
> and by which they were caught and made prisoners also.*
>
> —Volkert Evertsz, 1662

We watched them walking toward us, bobbing their heads,
black feathers waving like a flag; they were walking toward
a future they'd never get to walk out of—a future of changes
done to every landscape, riveting clouds of steel over every
inlet, river, bay. We watched them walking toward us.
Caught one, twisted its leg till it cried out. Watched the
others run from trees. Watched them twisting in our nets.
We used them up, their breaths bubbling, bodies to the sea.
We twisted words and feelings, doomed them for irredeemable
gestures of loyalty, Carolina parakeets easier to kill when they
were flocked around their dead. We reward the selfless hero;
we will not reward the dodo. We reward our own emotions,
but we use them in most animals. We use them to defend
what we've always known, what we've always been afraid
of: that the using of your kindness is the worst way of turning
your empathy against you until you're broken in two ways,
and nothing that you know of can ever repair them both.

Pacific Islands Under New Management

Galapagos penguins, eggs incubating
in a smoking crevice, hop over ropey

basalt dotted with sunning marine
iguanas and flightless cormorants.

They make a living on the back of
Fernandina after invasive species,

human encroachment, erased them
on other islands—how we lost twenty

species on Mauritius when sailors
sought to replicate fields of tea

and sugarcane—rats, cats, and stoats
jumping from their ships like picked

lice. Their numbers not as low as the
flightless kakapo, with few remaining,

or the greater short-tailed bat, which
walked on its wings to evolve in

reverse till its wings were almost
vestigial, like penguins who lost

their flight when they took to the sea.
A bird that became a fish, almost,

coming up drowned in fishing nets,
or scratching together a living in the

crevices of Fernandina in shrinking
numbers. It's why New Zealand was

silenced of birdsong, birds of paradise
declining in their ranges on Papua New

Guinea. The troubling question of
what we do to fix the Darwinian tide

of progress in the face of so much
diaspora. Island species were all once

imports too, worn on the backs of
tides till trapped on tiny seamounts.

Islands seldom getting new species
before the flush of Europeans and

their clinging leeches. The dodo,
mamo, auk mere casualties to progress,

a manifest destiny of carelessness.

Natural History Museum

Great Auk

Now we have whole prisons dedicated to the lost. We call these *habitat dioramas*, these memories of what has passed. Only we put the others on display. Our own, we bury, we give away to the earth. We don't make *example* and call it *ecosystem*. Surrounded by concrete, painted walls, verdant shades of ugliness, are malformed specimens: a great auk over plastic eggs, its glass eyes leaden and dull—less dead, and still more dead, than everything around it.

Eskimo Curlew

Now we have whole prisons dedicated to the lost. We call these habitat dioramas. We call them *death-in-life* as art. We don't care enough to name them. It's enough to have them standing in at all: *Eskimo curlew, possibly extinct, last authentic record.* It does not matter that we killed them because we did not name them, did not make them personal to us. We saw the aggregate, the amalgam stand-in, the whole collapsed race. It does not matter that even deer have distinct personalities to the researchers who study them—how our lives are not interchangeable, so why should theirs be? That this is how an animal goes extinct—this othering. This inability to see each loss on a personal level because each loss is not personal to you.

Spectacled Cormorant

Now we have whole prisons dedicated to the lost. We call these *habitat dioramas*. Each painted scene is cast in bas-relief against an artificial stillness. Stuffed birds in comical poses—a spectacled cormorant's neck bent like a scythe—an erudite gesture of *Dinosauria* before badly-painted water and lush forest. The dead awash in exposure as photogenic negative—unwilling as in flux—the reverse of film's intention—that these lookalikes cannot stand in for the living no matter how much we try to make them, not even as apologia or placard for our guilt. The scenery cannot take us from this statuary to something moving, cannot breathe the salt air over us, the sea wailing beyond us; it will not get us to remember something lost. When an animal is lost, it's lost forever. The museum becomes an unlikely cemetery for all our buried hopes, all the worlds we couldn't save. The words we could have said to them unspoken in our throat.

Daguerreotype, 1926

The last man
to hunt a thylacine
wept with grief

when he
was taken
to the crude hut

where he trapped them
with his father
as a boy.

He remembers
the *yip-yip* sounds
they made

when circling
the walls—
never-ending curiosity

never ending well.
He remembers taming one,
leading it around by rope,

a wooden pull toy—
specimens in museums
sometimes had

collar marks.
He was weeping
for the wrong reasons

for the feel
of something
not of something missing

the empty cave
we found inside
the last thylacine

thrown into
the dump the day
after it died.

II.

Pigeon of Passage

The Pigeon

of Passage

and the Red Oak—

the vanished

and the vanishing

collapsed habitat

collapsing

suspiciously Edenic.

Stilted stays[3]

inside

two figures:

pallid

slate gray

head &

open mouths

of faded leaves,

their marginal

teeth;

straight-back

chair

as diorama—

rigid

inflexible

drama.

---

[3] Corset.

Triptych on a Passenger Pigeon in 1886 Chicago

1.

Who
can be blamed

for the
extinction
of the
passenger pigeon?

I would be
no different

if I lived
back then:

a product of my
generation.

Nature:
perpetual, inexhaustible

a thing
unable to
be extinguished.

I would believe
the same
stupid logic.

Would think
shooting 20,000 birds
was good sport.

Would
have had
no problem

when they were
left to rot
in the dirt.

I would
have
extinguished you too.

It's why I
grieve
now.

I can
conceive
of a past

where
I fail you—

where
I keep

failing you.

2.

Only in death
              did you lay still,
always
         perpetually restless,

now your carcass
              gathers dust
in a drawer
              among specimens
in locked
              white cabinets,
hoping
              to change
the past by
              collecting
a piece of it,
              as if tamping
down dust
              over time
negates its
              passage—
or you only
              existed for
a moment
              and it can be
quantified
              in some way,
can be mastered—
              but your
beak is
         tatted and ripped,

your feathers
              weighted
with lime.
              Even time
keeps
         burying you—

only we
              hold onto

what we could
              not save.

3.

I can only
see you dead
in the past.

I try to imagine
you in the

Chicago market
you were
found in,

but all I see
is your body
ovate in

the dim lump
shape of
the dead—

your gorget's
iridescent sheen

glittering
strangely,
almost a star,

crusted with
coral and
bright magenta,

unfaded above
jagged feet
curled up, inward

like a bird
at the bottom
of a cage:

"The
      cat did it."

But don't we always
do that?

Blame others
when we left it
with the cat?

I mourn you
as if
I would have

done something
different.

That
future guilt
is enough

to save the past,
but
      it's not.

I would have
shot you too—

had you stuffed,
felt listlessly
indifferent

about
your absence
from the landscape,

lived as if you
never mattered,

because you
didn't.

The lives of others

never matter
so much
as we think—

we

don't matter
either.

The Mouth of Extinction

Sometimes I
wonder

about the careless
everything

I eat or are
eaten by others.

What lives do
I extinguish

that matter or
that mattered once?

Granted, I'm not
about to change

my behavior,
and these

are generalizations,
but I worry when

I read about
pigeons baked in

pie crusts and feel
my mouth water.

Is it wrong
to wonder

what an extinct animal
tasted like

if it was eaten
into extinction?

I must be Teddy Roosevelt
as presidency:

shoot it
skin it
& wear it

& then
preserve it.

Extinction 101

The owners of
                    extinct animals
loved them,
                    tamed them,
gave them names,
                    made them family pets.

We want to be close
                        to an animal
even if it results
                    in its death.
We want to feed
                    deer now

even if they're easier
                    to kill later
by hunters.
                    We want to take
away their wildness,
                    make them
less themselves,
                    to live with us
and make us happy.

                    I don't know
what love is
                    when I say this
(who has all
                    the answers),
but I know
                    it's not
using an animal
                    at the expense
of the animal.
                    We might be
the loneliest animal
                            when we do this;
                    we are
certainly the
                    most selfish.

Victorian Menagerie

We put whole stuffed birds
on hats, tiny hummingbirds
on bushels of egret feathers.

We held out for rarer species,
preserved birds of paradise
perched on wooden branches

or floating above bases using
wires, to adorn our libraries.
We collected dead menageries

of macaws and finches, pink-
headed ducks, paradise parrots
with their tails outspread.

We recreated a foreign
place as an expression of our
wealth until those places

were entirely transplanted,
their animals wiped out,
their landscapes gone or

overrun by introduced species.
So much of what we made
for ourselves was at the

expense of everything
around us, even our wives,
our servants—but we only

did what we really felt entitled
to, which is to say that we
did anything we wanted.

White Rhino, 2018

You remember its death,
                           the last white rhino,
but only as your guilt.
                           The world moves forward
without it, you
                           move forward. It's distressing
how easy it is
                           to forget, to look away
as life is ending or
                           to love it too much
and wrongly, to make it
                           into Instagram post
to show you really
                           care, while your cat
is killing songbirds,
                           a tiny gold-winged
warbler in its mouth,
                           one life overvalued,
one life undervalued.
                           You can't care only
when it suits you,
                           when statistics are easy
and easy to digest.
                           If each life matters,
then each life matters,
                           even if you have to make
hard choices, even if
                           caring means the world
you love is closing in
                           around you.

Black Rhino, 2011

You say that harming
                    an animal
with a small brain,
                    little knowledge,
little understanding,
                    does not absolve us
our cruelty,
                    that you can see
who we really are
                    by how we treat
the meanest
                    below us,
by what dismal speck
                    we hold
our power over,
                    or by how easily
we resolve our feelings
                    of terror
over the death
                    of something valuable.

But we're just trying
                    to make a living,
trying to use the land
                    we've always used,
and when we do so,
                    we are punished,
we're labeled
                    silent killer.
We're the men
                    that shot the rhino,
watched it drown
                    in its own blood.
We are the men
                    that watched
its orphaned calf
                    drink its rancid milk.

We are the men
              that left it
in a field
              as if a silent offering,
a prayer
              said for the sky.

Stool Pigeons

Even a wolf
in wolf's clothing
will still fool you,

even an agent
of your destruction
laid bare will still

entice. Even
flying over a long
sea of empty grass,

you will still land
in a trap set
with your kin—

turned traitor
to murder
their own future.

The live ones
slowly jerking
from the end

of a string,
wings gaping like
a gulping mouth.

Lashed to
the ground,
sometimes only

dummies,
the parched earth
spread with grain,

their wooden
bodies unmoved,
unmoving.

Still, you find
yourself landing
among them.

(The enemy within
is poisonous.
The exterior enemy

is merely foreign—
how a stranger seems
more hostile.)

Freedom
is not freedom
if you've chosen

your disaster—
is not the kind
of breakable mindset

you expect to
hold inside you
when the world

you know
is closing in
around you.

A Market Economy

We glutted the market with their bodies

till they were so cheap that
                        only the poor would eat them.

Till there were millions
                                no one would buy.

                        A sea of   unwanted pigeons
                            rotting in train cars became

a sea of   unwanted pigeons
                        in a Chicago or New York market

became a sea of   uneaten pigeons

dumped out on the grass
                from a Chicago or New York market

                        as landscape returned to us.

But you can't put things back
                when they are broken.

                        Even a child knows this.
You can't go back and
                return them.

Last Flight of the Wild Blue Pigeon (to Martha)

After your death,

                your body

was shipped

        by train

           to the Smithsonian

in a 300-pound

          block of ice.

Lying in state

        like Lincoln—

                countryside

flying by,

        becoming

                a brace of green.

Here you

        lived once

                died once.

The same train

        shipped you

                to markets,

shipped you

        to your death,

                carrying

the last of you

        onward.

                Or maybe

it's fitting

        to also go

                the same way

the others did,

        only your body

was alone.

Lost Animals

If we taxidermy
a person,

where does
the person go?

Just a rolled-out
empty skin suit

we salute
as carburetor.

Did a
passenger

pigeon hold a
carburetor too?

Was there
something to

salute so
I salute

a ghost or
what is left us

when I cry
over its carcass?

If I salute
the skin as

if a carburetor,
am I foolish?

This is the
only thing we

hold onto as if
it still exists.

Vestiary

You find yourself
preserving them,
holding them dear,

these vestibules
for bones, marble-
engaged tombs

covered with tacky
bas-relief of crowds
or holy figures.

You're living your
best life if you're
as lucky as the

worst loveless bastard
that got some carved
marble sundry for

him to lie under.
Even the unknown
bodies still get stones—

two headstones in
the cemetery near
my childhood home

were without names.
Each person has
the right to be

remembered briefly
and far away under
a pithy recondite—

even if only read

by local historians
or teenagers making

campy art projects,
still, someone sort
of remembers you—

someone inhabits
the space where
your name still lives.

I just want a place
where the name
of each lost animal

can live too. I want
an unknown grave
for every missing

species. I want a
marker to remind us
they are missing.

Isn't it obvious?
To respect an
animal means

mourning it with
the same respect
we mourn each other—

even the others
whose names we
cannot know.

Martha at the Smithsonian

On the 100-year anniversary of her death (imagine
the end of the *who* and the *what* of you), a rusty

brown specimen put out in a glass case for a new
memorial exhibit. *A celebration*, we said, *this form*

of going backwards. Holding up the body to believe
in as *hallelujah*, as what can save us and the earth

we all remember, the earth those we remember
still remember, the lumberjacks who posed with

twisted tree stumps (*look ma, four men deep!*) to
show how big they really were, to show how we

were overshadowed, the wonderment and the cruelty
of it (to be believed and to believe). We're still here,

though. We still have these thoughts, this conscious
loss. What does Martha have? What did her public

finally give her? A memorial her eyes can't see?
A reckoning of faith, still too late to save her?

Elegy for *Ectopistes Migratorius*

Ectopistes migratorius

means *wanderer*   *wanderer.*

You wandered   so far
away from
                the earth
that you disappeared. You
        took passage in   the canopy.
                Were swallowed in hectic   lightning.
The victim of   unlucky passage
        a passenger

                        the *wanderer*   *wanderer*—

            that
            which lives without

a home.

You were moving in 1869—
        flying over the Midwestern stratosphere
all top hats   and women's
millinery of egret feathers.
        Below you
people sweated and succeeded—   below you

the railroad buzzed with a new invention
                —splitting the country across   like a burst seam.

Steam spiraling up over the snake
                glittering strangely. A *wanderer*

                                        wanderer too—
made to be like you were—
        there is only one of you remaining.

                We don't respect what we don't make with our hands—
we are selfish that way.
                Now the snake moves   sleepily
where you used to move—   where you were streaking as a

        feathered river across the sky—
                a kind of railroad for passenger pigeons—

                        for the *wanderer*   *wanderer.*

Last Flight of the Wild Blue Pigeon

       Imagine pigeons

                        flocking

over you,

         tiny tufts
         of cloud—

from far away,

              the penciling

of bold wings,

            shadows
         falling,

patches of

         sun-dappled snow

as shining

           scales,

the blue

           and the
           blue-gray

cloud

         of wings.

NOTES

I.

POETRY COLLECTIONS are often monolithic. I consider this book, how-
ever, to be the work of many minds, including the countless books and
articles I readily absorbed in search of a voice that felt comfortably
mine while also maintaining scientific and historical authenticity to the
scholars and experts in those fields. I got into the magpie-like habit of
collecting information from conversations with park rangers, scientists,
archivists, and historians. I made notes about the species and subspecies
of animals, plants, vertebrates, and invertebrates. I wanted to know
the names of everything whose questions I felt poetry could answer.

Most of all, I wanted to do my best to accurately represent the sci-
ence and history that stood inside each poem, the dark green veins of
leaves when they are held up to the light. This has occasionally limited
the options with which I might describe a subject but has hopefully
left me less susceptible to the kind of problematic embellishment
that poets have sometimes adopted. As Emerson says in his essay on
self-reliance, "I will stand here for humanity, and though I would make
it kind, I would [also] make it true."

II.

THE POEMS FROM THE FIRST SECTION were written during residencies
at the Oregon Caves National Monument, the Cape Disappointment
State Park (Sou'wester Arts), the Morley Nelson Snake River Birds of

Prey National Conservation Area, and The Rice Place, respectively, and reflect the character of those areas. "Lost Object," "The Forest Took You Over," "Lost Sound (Spotted Owl)," "Listen Well (Sound Map)," "Terra Incognita," "Giant Redwood," and "Historical Graffiti" owe their impetus to the coastal forests of California, Oregon, and Washington.

"Last Prayer of the Logger" is an ekphrastic poem about an archival photograph of loggers from the Ericson Collection at the library of Cal Poly Humboldt. "How They Met Themselves" is loosely based on a Dante Gabriel Rossetti painting of the same name. "Listen Well (Sound Map)" is a rendering of the sound maps used in soundscape ecology to capture the bioacoustics of an area. "Silent Forest" loosely references the *Smithsonian* article "Smithsonian Scientists Solve Puzzle of Dramatic Wood Thrush Decline." "Lost Giants of the Pacific Coast" and "Old-Growth in Decline" are about famous trees profiled in Robert Van Pelt's *Forest Giants of the Pacific Coast.*

III.

THE SECOND AND THIRD SECTIONS are indebted to archival photographs of extinct animals and the people who interacted with them, especially from Errol Fuller's *Lost Animals: Extinction and the Photographic Record*; poems inspired by the book include "Laughing Owl, 1909," "Greater Short-Tailed Bat, 1965," "London Zoo, 1864," "Mamo, 1892," "Priorities | Memento Mori," and "Daguerreotype, 1892."

"The Animals of Lost and Found" is about the fiber art of Chiba Inada and the mission statement of Revive & Restore, a genetics lab using CRISPR gene editing to clone a passenger pigeon. "Thylacine, 1933" was inspired by a silent film of the last thylacine at the Beaumaris (Hobart) Zoo, Aboriginal rock art, and the Mountain Goats song "Deuteronomy 2:10."

"Daguerreotype, 1832" was inspired by Tim Gallagher's *The Grail Bird: The Rediscovery of the Ivory-Billed Woodpecker* and paintings from Alexander Wilson's *American Ornithology.* "Last Sighting of the Dodo" and "Pacific Islands under New Management" were influenced by Errol Fuller's *Dodo: A Brief History* and David Quammen's *The Song of the Dodo: Island Biogeography in the Age of Extinction.* "Daguerreotype,

1926" was inspired by a story told by geneticist Michael Archer during his talk "How We'll Resurrect the Gastric Brooding Frog, the Tasmanian Tiger" at *TEDxDeExtinction* in 2013.

"Victorian Menagerie" was written about Walter Rothschild, who collected 300,000 bird skins during his lifetime, many of which are still displayed at museums around the world; it is also loosely based on *Menagerie: The History of Exotic Animals in England* by Caroline Grigson. "National History Museum" was inspired by habitat dioramas in the American Museum of Natural History and the book *Windows on Nature: The Great Habitat Dioramas of the American Museum of Natural History* by Stephen Christopher Quinn.

"Black Rhino, 2011" and "White Rhino, 2018" were written about photographs of the last male northern white rhino found in an article in the October 2019 issue of *National Geographic* (Ami Vitale's "What I Learned Documenting the Last Male Northern White Rhino's Death"); the species is now functionally extinct.

"Pigeon of Passage" is ekphrastic, inspired by "The Pigeon of Passage & The Red Oak" by Mark Catesby in *The Natural History of Carolina, Florida, and the Bahama Islands, 1722-1726*. "Last Flight of the Wild Blue Pigeon" references a 19th century journal entry describing a super-flock of pigeons (T. M., *St. Nicholas Magazine*, 1873). "Martha at the Smithsonian" references Chris Heller's 2014 article in *The Atlantic* ("Martha, the Very Last Passenger Pigeon").

Lastly, many of the poems were inspired by both Joel Greenberg's *A Feathered River Across the Sky: The Passenger Pigeon's Flight to Extinction* and a passenger pigeon I viewed in the specimen collections of The Peregrine Fund outside Boise, Idaho. Poems based on these sources include "Triptych on a Passenger Pigeon in 1886 Chicago," "The Mouth of Extinction," "Extinction 101," "A Market Economy," "Lost Animals," "Vestiary," "Last Flight of the Wild Blue Pigeon (To Martha)," and "Elegy for *Ectopistes Migratorius*."

ACKNOWLEDGMENTS

There are many people, institutions, and organizations I would like to thank for assisting me during the completion of this book. I would like to thank the Idaho Commission on the Arts, the National Endowment for the Arts, and the Alexa Rose Foundation for providing financial support in the form of four artist grants.

I would like to thank the editors who included poems in the following publications, sometimes in earlier forms: "Lost Object" in *Blueline Magazine*; "The Forest Took You Over" in *Camas Magazine*; "Last Prayer of the Logger" in the Death Rattle Writers Festival ekphrasis zine; "Mule Deer" in *EcoTheo Review*; "Terra Incognita" and "Giant Redwood" in *Plant-Human Quarterly*; "Historical Graffiti [3]" in *The Indianapolis Review*; "Historical Graffiti [4]" in *Glassworks Magazine*; "Lost Giants of the Pacific Coast" in *The Westchester Review*; "London Zoo, 1864" in *Word for Word*; "Daguerreotype, 1832" in *Wild Roof Journal*; "Martha at the Smithsonian" in *Under a Warm Green Linden*; "Mamo, 1892" and "Elegy for *Ectopistes Migratorius*" in *Anti-Narrative Journal*; "Last Sighting of the Dodo [1]" and "Natural History Museum [3]" in *Evening Street Review*; "Triptych on a Passenger Pigeon in 1886 Chicago" and "A Market Economy" in *The Wire's Dream Magazine (Black Lion Journal)*; "Last Sighting of the Dodo [3]" and "Natural History Museum [1]" in *Water*, an anthology published by Michigan State University; and "Greater Short-Tailed Bat" and "Priorities | Memento Mori" in *Where is the River :: A Poetry Experiment*. Additionally, I would like to thank Bill Ripley of Another New Calligraphy for publishing an excerpt from the manuscript in the chapbook *We Don't Bury Our Dead When Our Dead Are Animals.*

I am grateful to the following individuals and institutions who provided me with artist residencies that were instrumental to the manuscript: George Herring and the park rangers at the Oregon Caves National Monument; Corrine Coffman, Joseph Weldon, and the staff at the Morley Nelson Snake River Birds of Prey National Conservation Area; Sou'wester Arts, for providing a cabin to write about exploration in the Pacific Northwest; the Boise Public Library; and The Rice Place, for giving me the time and space to revise the project in later stages.

I am also grateful to the following organizations for providing venues to share my work while the project was still developing: Idaho Botanical Garden's BLOOM Reading Series, Storyfort, Campfire Stories, KRBX Radio Boise, MING Studios, Lit Youngstown, Death Rattle Writers Festival, The Cabin, SoulFood Poetry Night, and the Boise State University Department of Sustainability's Earth Day Reading Series.

Finally, I would like to thank the following people for assisting me in various ways: Daphne Stanford, Catherine Broadwall, Aurora Mehlman, Chris Mathers Jackson, Rebecca Evans, Megan Williams, Susan Lasater, Cathy Rodabaugh, and Lisa Brady all provided feedback, friendship, support, or advice. Curtis Evans and Tate Mason from The Peregrine Fund were kind enough to show me a passenger pigeon that was the project's impetus. Lastly, I would like to thank my partner Raymond for everything he does and has done to support me. I am lucky to have him.

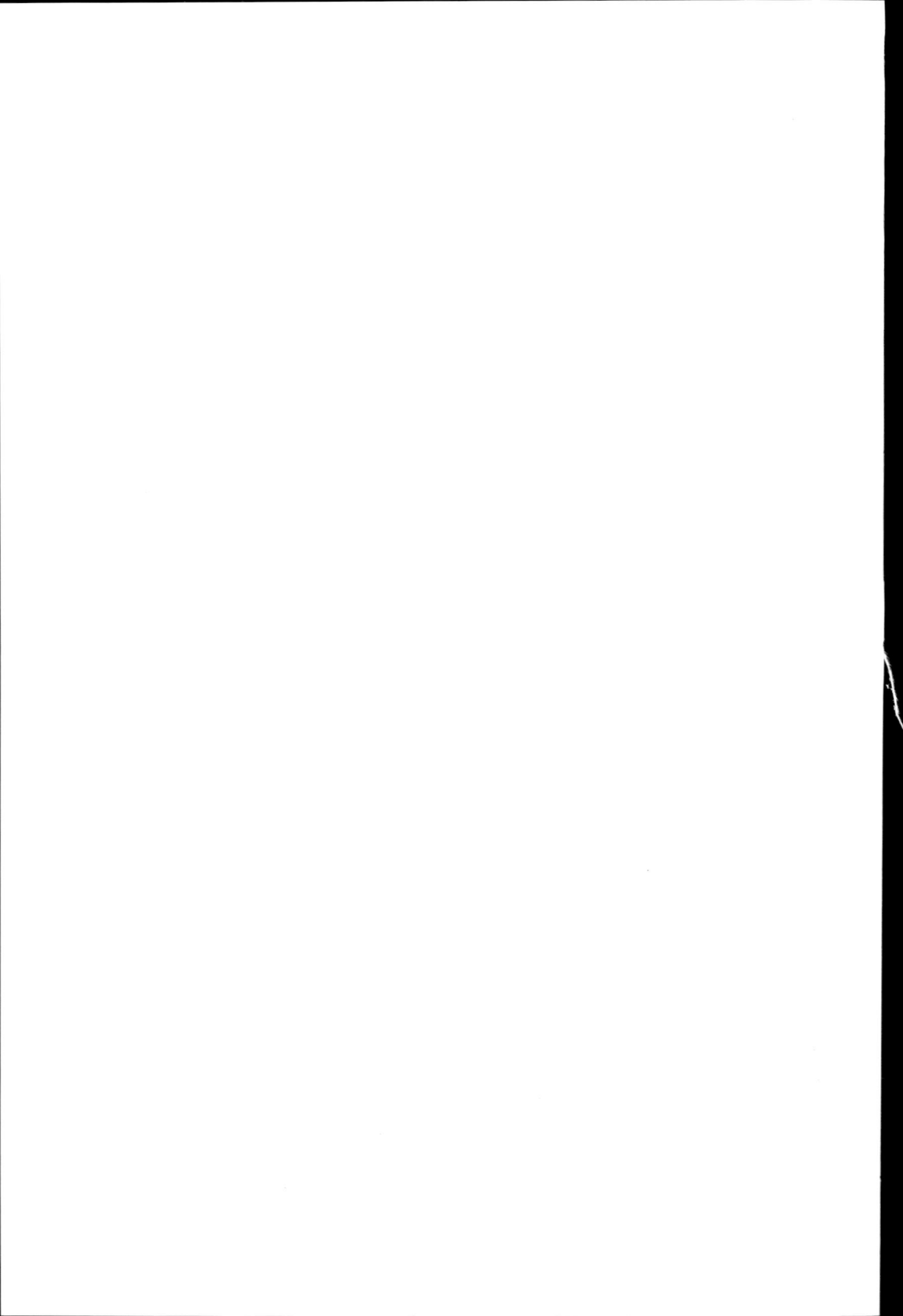

HANNAH RODABAUGH is the author of four chapbooks of poetry, including *We Don't Bury Our Dead When Our Dead Are Animals* and *The Leonids*. Her poetry has been featured in *The Indianapolis Review, Camas Magazine, Glassworks Magazine, Plant–Human Quarterly, The Westchester Review, EcoTheo Review,* and *Berkeley Poetry Review.* She is the recipient of a Literature Fellowship from the Idaho Commission on the Arts and has twice been an Artist-in-Residence for the National Park Service. She lives in Boise, Idaho where she teaches at Boise State University and the College of Western Idaho.

www.ingramcontent.com/pod-product-compliance
Lightning Source LLC
Chambersburg PA
CBHW022102020426
42335CB00012B/789